Mended Wings

Poetry of a Cancer Survivor

Jan Cox

"Mended Wings: Poetry of A Cancer Survivor," by Jan Cox. ISBN 978-1-62137-702-3 (Softcover).

Published 2015 by Virtualbookworm.com Publishing Inc., P.O. Box 9949, College Station, TX 77842, US.

Dedication

This book is dedicated to all those who have been a part of my healing journey.

This includes:

My husband who lived the journey with me, our daughter who made sure I got the best hospital and doctor care, our son who drove me to Commonweal and back and shaved his head for me, my sister Cheri who spent two weeks helping out after surgery and who created the beautiful cover for this book, my dear friends who were always there in so many wonderful ways, and the many beautiful people of the healing professions.

Foreword

One of the greatest joys in my life is to write poetry. As you open the pages of this book, written during and after two separate cancers, know that you are entering my heart, my soul, my being. It is with a wish for your healing or of someone you know that I present these poems as a story of what can happen and did. I hope they will speak to your heart, also.

Here you will find six sections, each section dealing with a specific aspect of this journey through cancer and beyond. The first three revolve around the original diagnosis, treatment and healing of the first cancer. The second three relate to my movement through a second cancer with an emphasis on growth toward wholeness.

Today I invite you along on this journey from diagnosis to healing, from difficulty to celebration, from the old me to the new.

REMARKABLE

You say I'm remarkable and
I wonder why? Is it because I
walked through cancer and
came out the other side?

So have more people than
you can count.

Is it because I've been
married 48 years and am
still lovingly present?

I haven't told you about
the ups and downs in
those long years.

Is it because I'm writing
poetry at 70 years old?

I know a woman who began
her life story at 90.

Is it because I listen
to my dreams and
continue to grow?

That is just one way
to know myself. Your way
may be different.

Is it because I'm a mother, a
daughter, a sister, a wife, a
giver, a helper, a doer, a
friend?

That is the way of most
women I have met.

Or....

Is it because I have
walked through cancer and
come out the other side
and that means you
can too?

Onset

A SEVEN MINUTE MAELSTROM

The phone rang and alone
I answered, listened, heart
pounding in my ears.

> *I'm sorry to tell you it's cancer he said.*

Ears heard. Heart
plunged, muscles like
jelly. Mind screamed
No, No. Voice whispered,
Is it true?

> *I'm sorry to tell you like this he said.*
> *It's Friday and I want you to know.*

Body sat and sat.

Disbelief swirled. Anger seethed.
Chaos reigned. Tears streamed
until calm finally fought its way
through and knowing settled in
while life's dreams exploded
into dust.

WAR

The President states
with self-assured inanity
*The only way to survive
is to be the toughest
to get them before
they get us!*

The oncologist announces
from the midpoint of his ego
*The only way to control
your cancer is to attack it
get it before it
gets you!*

My heart longs to believe
there is another way
a gentler way. But
while I seek for answers
the war in my body
has begun unbidden
and I am torn
apart.

CELLS GONE CRAZY

The room was bright with comfy
green chairs. Sunny nurse smiles
reached out, invited me into a
web of tubes and bags and
I smiled back, relaxing, and chose
a chair with a view outside where
flowers waved in the morning breeze.

A needle stick into the port, a few
quiet questions from the nurse, a
bag of clear poison connected
and I was ready.

A friend pulled up a chair, pulled
out Scrabble, and we began playing,
laughing, playing some more and
the nurses smiled while the bag
dripped the clear fluid slowly, slowly
hour after hour, hunting down those
cells gone crazy.

Others sat with eyes closed, some
talked quietly, some watched TV until
one man entered in his socks for the
day—bright, gaudy, oranges and reds
worn with a twinkle and a get well
wish not only for himself but all of us.

And laughter rippled through the room
slowly dripping into each body
leaving no room for those
cells gone crazy.

SURVIVING CHEMO

What else can I do
today but lie here
in my cat corner, curled
mewling, eyes turned
inward, brain short circuited.
My space has collapsed

into a pile of pillows warmed
by autumn sun melting me
deep into self. Not a black
hole. No. The beams of light
stay my fearsome phantoms
of death. I will survive

lying here drinking
in heat that burns off
the dross, toasting each
memory that forges new
strength in punctured
veins, dreaming of spring.

Struggle

HEART MUSIC

There are just some
days when the heart music
screeches to a halt and
refuses to add even one
more eighth note to the
symphony of a world
lost in itself, buried
under the complexity
of being.

HOT FLASH

What is this that invades
my being in waves leaving
no pleasure, only the
intense rage of molten
lava setting me afire.

I long to settle into a cooling
silence, listening, creating,
but it begins again and yet
again and always again.

Formed in a distant turbulence
deep in the interior
of my being it rushes
upward from this
hellfire warming the room
around me.

Stripping me of all
protective cover it reddens
face without embarrassment
condenses on angry brow
creating embers of
irritation that slowly die
out in a cooling rush
of welcome wind.

CHEMO BRAIN

People rush in to fill the
silence when the right word
just gets lost.

> *Aggravation!*

Others politely wait, hoping
the word will be found
in time for lunch.

> *Embarrassment!*

The burner is bright red
although the food has long
since been served.

> *Fear!*

What did I come to this room
to do? I know it was important.

> *Frustration!*

Someone left a message
for you. Now where
did I put it? Who was it? What did
they want?

> *Exasperation!*

What is your name again? Why
can't I remember?

Vexation!

Chemo brain you say? You
are just learning about it? It
affects the brain cells?
It will get better?

Relief!

Healing

I BROUGHT THE LUNCH

When the walls began
closing in and life was
out there, she piled me
into her car with her dog, our
cameras, sunscreen and hats
and we made our way into a
different world, one of sunshine,
green meadows, singing streams and
corn flowers. We walked with
the wind, laughed in the sun,
photographed mountains, breathed
the clear air and the walls
disappeared. I brought
the lunch.

MY UNQUIET HEART

I feel
my unquiet heart
unfold, siphoning off
entrancement, kinked
composure, tangled filaments
of bleary-eyed tenacity.

I feel
my unquiet heart
unbridle, nibbling remote
reams of dawn pink
sensing euphoria
behind greening glimpses
of hope.

I feel
my unquiet heart
murmuring misty
messages of release
waxing lavishly
wearing fully a
hard won joy.

GO

I have become my own
therapist, spinning invisible
wings to embrace the neon
GO diligently inscribed on the
living room of my soul.

Breathless I fly over the
Zambezi and on to Pom-Poko.
My rendezvous with Moon
slows serrated breath, fills the
lingering vacuum with thundering
calm, luminous luxury, and
vermillion canyons—a six
minute paradise.

THE LAMP

I remember the day
you arrived, tissue wrapped
in a simple shopping bag
delivered in love by one
with knowing heart and
helping hands.

I clutched the open door in
disbelief, hardly breathing for
fear that this moment would
vanish in a dream, and you
with it.

But, you remain. And I remain.

Your beaded shade, blues
and greens of spirit and growth
your classic calming contours
your place by my rocker
your light drawing me to
return day by day, breath by
breath, cell by cell, until
filled with your afterglow, this
body now shines in
serene gratitude.

Return

RERUN

A distant land called
and we stepped out in
joy. New Zealand's beauty
captured our wandering
hearts, filled our days with
healing, sent us soaring
overtook concern. We loved,
we played, we dreamed, we danced
and we flew home sated.

Then the nightmare began. My
return became a rerun, a doctor
again said *cancer* and my world
grew small.

Anger captured this worn body
clawing at the cancer cage. Rage
stomped its feet, frantic, frenzied,
hysterical until encircled in the arms
of friends I began to breathe, in....
out....in....out....in.....out...and hope
peeked into the door of my heart
once more.

DISRUPTION

I sit in silence in this
still small space
calm, cool, clean and
quiet while just beyond
these walls the world of
frenzied movement
threatens my being.

I resist going forth into
the voracious mouth of life
to be swallowed up by
other's agendas, desires, and
disruptions leaving no
room for one who desires
only peace.

WILLING LIFE

A winding path filled with
roadblocks rose up before me
with no turning back, no mistake
to be claimed and forgiven.
Just facts. Cancer had come
to call again.

Breasts which had once
fed a child, tempted a mate
turned on me ready to
kill this body, this being.
Darkness arose. Death dawdled
nearby filling my days with
fear and foreboding.

Then came the fierce NO shouted
from the center of my deepest
Self. I will not succumb to this
nightmare. And a gentler YES
followed. I will stand and fight. I will
lose my parts for the sake of the
whole. I will do whatever it takes.
I want to live.
       I will live.
          I will.

HAVE YOU GRIEVED?

Sitting in the warmth of her wood
heated living room, my friend listened
quietly as I poured forth anger,
frustration and emptiness. *Why?*
I questioned—my ribs sore, my chest
numb, my mind in chaos at the loss
of what once fed my baby boy, excited
my husband, made me feel like a woman.
Now all that was left were scars that shouted
from the mirror—cancer— you are
no longer you, whole, complete.

When my friend's eyes met mine,
she asked, *Have you grieved, my friend,
have you grieved?*

My eyes filled with tears as I shook my head
no.

That day, I carried her question home
in my heart, feeling all the sadness
anger, loss, letting the tears fall
and fall and fall until grief
resolved itself into acceptance and
grew into thanksgiving for a
life still to be lived.

Emergence

AWAKENING

Toxic thoughts race through
this mind, planted there by one
who bullies, belittles, ignores, and
competes. Entering the inner
recesses of this body, they
weaken will, overpower love,
dampen spirit, erase Self.
I cringe
      I mourn
            I dream

Awakening I know
this need not be. I am who I am,
imperfect, sensitive, loving, forgiving,
creative and whole. This
ambushed mind stills while an
inner song fills my being, singing to
Self, watering spirit, restoring
will, and returning love.
Once again I am at peace.

EXPECT A MIRACLE

One night, inner chaos
stopped, held its breath
and listened....

Deep in the dark recesses
behind the monkey mind there
arose a soft and velvet
whisper.
> *Miracles happen;*
> *Now, here*
> *in a dream, a poem*
> *a word, a vision*
> *in a flash.*

And then....

a new note reverberates
through every living cell.

> All is possible. It is
> not decreed. Life can
> continue until all is
> said and done and
> time releases its hold
> as gently as a feather
> floating on the winds of
> eternity.

THE ACUPUNCTURIST

He came to town riding
his white steed, prepared
for the fight and I spoke to
him and he spoke to
me and he cared.

He poked and prodded
grinned and digressed
listened and learned
a needle here, a needle
there, a question here,
suggestion there.

And through the years
he watched as hope
returned and celebrated
as healing blossomed
then once again rode off
on his white steed to
discover new lands where
others were waiting
patiently for his
healing gift.

EMERGING

Once, when ash blond
overlaid gray strands
and chemicals created
curls the world was perhaps
fooled into believing life
could continue by dint
of imagination, will and
wishful thinking.

But no more.

Now as baby soft
curls begin to warm this
hairless head, others
grin and run fingers
through the down.
Look, they say, *You're
curly! How did that happen?*

And I reply
*By going through the
fire and emerging
on the other side.*

They nod as if
they understand this
curly badge of courage.

Some do. Others will.

Now I wear my years
in truth counting
hours, days and hairs
on my head in
gratitude.

HIDDEN AWAY

Her days were pleasant, filled
with housework, cooking,
eating, talking, laughing,
reading, play while her heart
hidden away behind her
rainbow sweater and her flat
chest beat loudly, insistently,
irregularly at times.

Under the covers
a burning would spread over
that heart—a heat radiating
outward to distant limbs
a touch of anger attached
nagging at her, forming
a question.

Why?

Until that night, the recent
one, anger emerged through the
heat, consuming her dreams
rousing her mind, flowing
volcanically from heart to
distant cells, spewing forth
all that was hidden, tamped
down, refused, ignored, until

she lay watching herself beat the
pillow, scream at the jays
stomp her feet and finally give
voice to that which was
hidden away in the recesses
of her heart.

Spirit rejoiced as she handed
it over and cool again,
she slept soundly once more
a smile in her heart.

THE HOMEOPATH

He entered her life one
day and knowing she
had much hard work
to do, hesitantly agreed
to help her heal.

A scientist of sorts, he
searched her psyche for
the right remedy with the
power to clear out debris
from the war that had taken
place within her body.

He spoke a 200 year old
language of health, new to
this soul who listened, learned
followed and healed—body
mind and spirit. And strength
returned, dark became light while
fear turned to faith, and
wholeness abounded.

Daily she moves forward
living moment by moment
basking in the beauty
of a new peace, drinking at
the font of gratitude.

Rebirth

REALITY REVISITED

In my body lies a miasma
of words, thoughts, emotions
unsettled feelings birthed
from past traumas seeping forth
and controlling who I hope
to be in this lifetime.
But, just today I realize I no
longer have to accept such
reality just because it once
was; I no longer need to
feel those experiences
listen to those thoughts
accept that reality as best
for this body, this life
or this spirit.

COMING INTO BEING

Out of the depths
where foul stenched
garbage resolves itself
into compost, a new
viewpoint sprouted
> pushed through the soil
> laid down by life's struggles
> soaked up the sun through
> a break in the fog
> waved in the warm wind of
> imagination and bloomed.

Possibility prodded the
senses into a Yes!
Fresh-faced, eyeing the
big picture, she grasped the
contradiction and knew
> to be accepted, accept
> to be loved, love
> to be whole, BE.

LOOK!

Indigenous to this
cock-eyed world is
the not so subtle myth that
we must go to extremes to
show our power. We live
in terror that if we yield
that power, that control, that
world view, we will be less than,
nothing, lost, overtaken.

But Look!

I am weary of shadow selves, of
contradictions that suggest
to find peace we must fight, to
stay alive we must kill, to Be
we must dominate when
the radical answer lies
outside fear.

Look!

The heart knows a shift
must come—a shift to
love; mysterious love
        courageous love
        outrageous love
        immediate love.

CLEANING HOUSE

Buried deep within my
body are a multitude
of voices, echoing numerous
authorities who believe
they have the answers
for how to live my life *if only I*
would listen, learn, emulate.
Now, one by one I will them
away, unchain them from that
vault of *shoulds,* liberate them from
the cells which hold them, unlock
the door to freedom and sweep
them out. And when they
attempt to enter again, which
they always do, I will watch
and wait, unattached, to see
where they intend to hide
and quickly whisk them
out once more.

A CALLING

The coast calls....visions
of delicious discovery send
sudden urges through this
closet gypsy. Time for
stress relief, pleasure, the
wise world of wave and
wonder. Therapy that
delights, enlightens, dances its
way through blood and
fiber. Connects. I go,
spinning off yesterday, reaching
for mystery, foggy footing,
windblown delight. I spread
my mended wings and fly.

THE MOMENT

Alone, I return
to the one who knocks
on this heart door
begging to enter and
remain for an hour
or maybe a lifetime.

Whispers of words pushed
under a barrel where no
light can shine forth
and create havoc
slip out from a crack
ready to return.

And I laugh pure joy
at their return, heart
expanding outward in a
fireworks display unequaled
in past independence day
extravaganzas.

THE NAMING

My mother thought
my name was her—Frances
with an "e"—good girl,
perfect replica of a
demanding discipline.

But my grandpa named me
Free Bear, embracing the
spark that lolly-gagged
within and danced
around my eyes.

My mother named me
Daughter, pink zinnia in
a sedate flower bed lined
with cement.

But my grandpa twinkled
me, Running Wild Willow,
weaving through scorn and
frown, bursting forth through
whisker rub and belly laugh.

Now I claim myself
born of immense fire
shooting skyward from sultry
cosmic cataclysm.

And in the solitude of my
midnight dreams, that fire names me
Passion, Intensity, Rage, Joy,
Breathless Being. And I
dance at my naming.

IN GRATITUDE

Today I awake to sun glinting
through curtains, promising a day
of play, laughter and joy.

Today I awake to rain on the roof
beating a tempo of reading,
rest, beauty and peace.

Today I awake to fog hiding the
world, bringing close the gift
of meditation and mindfulness.

Today I awake with gratitude surging
through this body, creating release
to my soul and pure acceptance.

Tomorrow I shall awake again and
again, until tomorrows cease, and each
one a gift to this grateful being.

Afterword

Dear Reader,

For those of you who would like a little more information about my cancer journey, I invite you to read on. I have talked to many survivors since becoming one, and each will say the same thing. Cancer taught me so much. But I am getting ahead of myself. First let me tell you a little more about who I am and about this cancer journey.

Growing up, cancer was a very scary word in our family. My mother's mother died from it when my mom was 3 years old. This affected my mom throughout her life. It was so hard for her when Dad died from congestive heart failure in 1999 following a deep brain stroke seven years earlier. Mom died the following year. In 2002, I was diagnosed with cancer and was so thankful this diagnosis came after their deaths. I remember being asked if anything difficult had happened in my life about two years earlier. I had to say yes. I was my parents' long distant caretaker, traveling often between California and Wisconsin, taking care of their paper work, their hospital and their nursing home stays.

When diagnosed in 2002, I was shocked. It was a small virulent lump at the base of my right breast. I discovered it myself. All of a sudden I had to find an oncologist and there were none where we lived. We drove 80 miles to a larger city down a long winding mountain road to meet doctors recommended by a local surgeon who had done my biopsy. Soon I had a team of doctors, each doing his or her part to help me heal. When I began chemotherapy, the chemo nurses became my heroes. I cannot praise these nurses highly enough. They do an amazing job working with patients while keeping our fear at bay.

Throughout chemotherapy and radiation, many people stepped forward to offer food, rides, cards, gifts, prayers and any kind of help that was needed. That was tremendously humbling. Sometimes people would stay with me for hours as the chemo dripped into my veins through a port. We played games and talked and laughed and the time went quickly. Then, after chemo and before the upset stomach began, we would have a great lunch in one restaurant or another before heading back up the mountain.

That year, I was working as a reading teacher of first graders in a small school district. I worked when I could and took sick days when I was too ill from the side effects to be at work. I used all of my saved sick days in one year. And I was again humbled when several fellow teachers offered me some of their days in case I ran out. I was thankful that I didn't have to use this generous offer. Teaching was always a love of mine, but by 2004 I knew that I needed to retire somewhat early in order to heal faster.

Several things helped that healing. From my research, I felt a strong sense of a need for complementary medicine along with chemo and radiation. A young doctor of Functional Medicine arrived in a nearby town and became my acupuncturist and my cheerleader. His reputation preceded him and I think I was his first patient. He was there throughout both cancers.

A good friend and cancer survivor suggested I work long distance with doctors from Pine Street Clinic in San Anselmo who set up a protocol of vitamins, minerals and Chinese medicines. I jumped at the chance to receive help from them. My own doctor teamed up with them to gain more knowledge and use their suggested acupuncture. All this was done through phone calls.

Chemo, radiation, prayer, meditation, visualization, diet, exercise, reading, and writing all played a part in my healing and finally one day, I was ecstatic to learn that the cancer had completely disappeared, "gone into remission," they said, and we celebrated.

In fact we celebrated in the winter of 2006-07 by heading to Australia and New Zealand for a seven week stay. After two weeks of amazing sights in Australia including Sidney, Uluru and the Outback, and the Great Barrier Reef, we headed to New Zealand. Here we rented a camping van and traveled both islands, soaking up this laid back culture, relaxing, laughing, exploring, and just feeling good to be alive.

Returning home, and looking in a mirror for the first time in weeks, I noticed a worrisome rash on my left breast. It was several weeks before I could get into the oncologist to be checked out. When I did, his words cut right through my happiness. "Oh no, I think this is Inflammatory Breast Cancer." IBC is fairly rare and also virulent. As a result, he moved quickly and I was right back in chemotherapy once again. The oncologist was usually careful with his words, but this time he said, "Your breasts are killing you," and I took him at his word and had a double mastectomy followed by more radiation and chemo. That was 8 years ago.

As we discussed my possible death, a huge desire to live arose within me. Once again I added complementary therapies to my daily regimen. And this time I went to Commonweal, a beautiful retreat center at the ocean, near Bolinas, California. Here, eight survivors met for a week of caring for our bodies in every way you could imagine. Together we ate scrumptious vegetarian meals while talking and sharing. We had a one-on-one appointment with an amazing psychologist who gave her time to this cause; and another talk with Michael Lerner, well known author and co-founder with Rachel Naomi Remen of the Commonweal Cancer Help Program. We walked, danced, and did yoga each morning. We were given three massages during the week. We talked, we wrote, we cried, and we healed. And once more I survived. For those interested in this integrative care support group, please go to www.commonweal.org.

There are many ways to build up the immune system after going through cancer therapies. I happened on a homeopath who came to a local business to speak about homeopathy. I was intrigued and began working with him to repair my immune system and to rid my body of the toxins left from the treatments. My body began healing and getting stronger and stronger. I began looking well and feeling well.

In summary, one makes lots of personal discoveries when going through cancer. First and foremost I discovered that I need to take time for and give more energy to myself, and that doing so is not selfish. I have learned how to receive love and care from others with sincere gratitude. I have learned that in order to live fully I need to let go of worries about how I am perceived by others. I know now that I have little control over many things in life but what is important is how I respond to the problems that arise. I have learned to trust my spiritual life as being right and good and healing for me. I have developed a deeper understanding of God and God's place in my life. I have learned to forgive myself, to take myself less seriously and to spend more time laughing and being joyful. And I have learned to be grateful for every day I am alive. Finally, the best learning of all is that on some days I forget everything I have learned. And that is OK, too!

Jan